My Travelling Spirit

by
Carly Morrison

Folioavenue Publishing Service
Level 33, Australia Square 264 George Street Sydney,
Australia 2000 (800) 9866796
www.folioavenue.com

Copyright © 2021 by Carly Morrison

All rights reserved. No part of this book may be used or reproduced by any means, graphic, electronic, or mechanical, including photocopying, recording, taping or by information storage retrieval system without the written permission of the author except in the case of brief quotations embodied in critical articles and reviews.

Because of the dynamic nature of the internet, any web addresses or links contained in this book may have changed since publication and may no longer be valid. The views expressed in the work are solely those of the author and do not necessarily reflect the views of the publisher, and the publisher hereby disclaims any responsibility for them.

Printed in Australia

ISBN: Paperback: 978-1-951795-20-7

Chapter 1

Take care of you

Since the age of 13, I was already surrounded by women who read tarot cards and performed psychometry. Psychometry is the art of giving a psychic reading while holding a piece of jewelry the client was wearing. I recall having a reading at the age of 13 where the reader told me: ***"You have the gift of intuition & throughout your life it will be a blessing and a curse".***

Boy was she right! No truer words have ever been spoken to me. I am now in my late forties. I have my own business called Psychic Dreaming. Basically, I perform Reiki, Theta and Serenity vibrational healing for my clients.

All my life I have had a love of crystals and magic, and I decided to write my book to share some of the most amazing spiritual experiences that I have had throughout my life!

I would like to start by explaining the extra sensory perceptions or ESPs that people can possibly experience. The first one is clairvoyance, {Clear sight}. A clairvoyant is a person with the gift of clairvoyance. Someone who receives extrasensory impressions and symbols in the form of mental images through their mind's eye, or the third eye.

Claircognizance, is a feeling in which you just suddenly know something to be true. You didn't see it, hear it or feel it - you just know it.

Clairaudience (clear hearing) means being able to perceive sounds, words or noise from the spiritual realm. Yes, we are talking about hearing voices, either outside yourself or inside of your head.

Clairempathy (clear emotion) is the ability to sense other people's emotions, thoughts and symptoms. It is the awareness or perception of a person's emotional state, without even asking them.

Claircentience (clear physical feeling) is when you obtain intuitive insight by way of a physical feeling in their body, i.e. gut feeling.

Clairtangency (clear touching) is the ability to perceive facts about an event or person by contact or proximity to the object or person. This is also commonly known as psychometry.

Clairsalience (clear smelling) involve insights coming through smell, like smelling your grandmother's perfume out of the blue and knowing that she is reaching out to you from the spiritual realm.

Clairgustance (clear tasting) is receiving psychic information through the sense of taste.

The reason I have explained these is that throughout my life. I have experienced predominantly clairaudience. Due to being honest about hearing voices. I have been hospitalized, confined and locked up 10 times, as psychiatry doesn't account for these senses and labels this as auditory hallucinations which it isn't.

In the times of my confinement. I just meditated and chanted silently in my head. While this event in my life was extremely challenging, I believed that every experience we go through has a lesson.

The first time I was hospitalized was when I was 27 years old. It was a major lesson in acceptance. I was in solitary confinement and just being viewed through a window. In the beginning, I was fighting the whole reality, and banging on the door yelling at them to let me out. It was only at the point that I came to full acceptance of my predicament and stopped fighting it that they came in and said I could go. A year after being discharged, I saw an amazing astrologer in Perth. He summed up my experience in the first five minutes of meeting him. He asked me about a year ago: "Did you think that you could read people's minds and knew what they were thinking? Also you could tell if people were lying to you?" I told him yes!

He also said in my astrological chart. I have four planets in Pisces, and they all kicked into activation. So that is what he described is exactly what happened to me!

Let's move on and talk about something completely different. My first love passed away at a young age. By the time that he died, we were no longer in contact and living in different states in Australia. For one whole week, I would dream of being with him every night. In those dreams, he would be hugging me and stroking my hair, telling me how much he loved me.

Each morning, I would wake from this dream feeling that his spirit was no longer here on Earth and I would just cry. At the end of that year, through a friend. I was reunited by phone with his sister. Over the phone I sang her the song Last Goodbye by Jeff Buckley. Which always made me think of her brother. She told me that, she always knew I was psychic. It turns out that, when her brother had died, she and his other sister would console each other by singing this exact song over the phone. They'd think of him while singing, and crying and sharing their memories with each other.

Another very close friend of mine also passed in the following year. Before his death, I had a nightmare that a different friend was driving under the influence, after which he crashed and, soon after, died. Upon waking from this dream. I couldn't let it go and had the strongest feelings one of my friends would be passing but I didn't know who at the time. Naturally I was very upset by this dream. A few weeks after this dream I discovered my intuition was correct and one of my friends had indeed passed away.

On a separate occasion. When I was hospitalised. In the morning, while having breakfast, I happened to look at the young man sitting at the table opposite me. Whilst I was looking at him. There was a point, I saw a yamaka on his head, but it vanished after I gave him a second look. I asked him about it. He told me that a past life regressionist once told him. That in one of his past lives. He was a

Jewish priest! So that explained my vision!

I also have always loved reading books about spirituality and manifesting. I recently finished reading "super attractor" by Gabby Bernstein. Whilst reading it I realized that I have always done it. I had manifested my dreams becoming my reality like my first trip to India, or my travels in Thailand, Malaysia, Singapore, Indonesia, and, now, a book deal.

It's all just a matter of journaling it, Stating it and believing it. Then it will come into being. You should also be grateful for where you currently have in your life. All we have is this now moment. So when you visualise and affirm something is already in your life. Soon after it naturally follows suit and comes into being in your life. If you dream it you can achieve it.

At the same time I started reading cards, I was also practicing white magic, white magic or Wicca as it is called. Wicca has a rule to harm no one, also not to interfere with anyone's free will.

Now, I perform the spells from a magical witch box spell once a month. A few months back the theme was luck, and this spell worked a treat! I won four competitions, with $5000 worth of various items and a scholarship. This month's theme is self-love which I will be performing on the full moon 14th October 2019. The full moon will be in my sign, Aries, so it's a usually good time for me.

Another ritual I perform daily is called smudging. To smudge correctly you must incorporate the four elements: a sage stick for the earth element and fire is there once the end of the sagestick is lit. An abalone shell for the water element, and a feather for the air element. The smoke represents the ether. I light the sage stick and hold it just above the abalone shell using my left hand, and then with the right hand wave the feather to lift the smoke around my body to cleanse and purify my energy. This is the way of smudging.

My life has been full of rituals. On my first trip to India, I was staying in Ahmedabad every day. During this time. I had to perform a daily puja ceremony. I had a statue of my deity, Mahakali Durga she is the goddess of the light. I would light the incense, present my offerings of fruit and flowers then wash the statue before prayers. I would then wash it with water then milk, and then anoint it with red powder and rice. I would have to share Prasad the fruit with all the neighbor's afterwards. I would often spend hours shopping for all the necessary items to be able to have everything and perform the puja correctly.

I was also lucky to have visited Ghandi's ashram in Ahmedabad. There, I meditated in his room. It was an amazing and profound experience for me. I couldn't believe I was standing in his room. It was a small room with a glass cabinet that held ashes, glasses, spinning wheel, clothes and shoes. On that day. I made a vow to myself to have as much positive impact on the world as possible.

I have also volunteered for activist work in the past. I would assist at phone banks to gain funding for the Australian conservation foundation in attempt to stop Adani. I don't want to see our wonderful Great Barrier Reef destroyed. Aside from phoning banks, I was also doing social media promotions of the events, as well as emailing and phoning certain ministries who are willing to work with Adani.

I firmly stand with the indigenous people or this land, and I am totally dumbfounded at this government's lack of care and concern for the many wonderful beautiful natural wonders that Australia has, the Adani mine is still an ongoing concern.

I also wish to encourage more people to take up the practice of Agni hotra at sunrise and sunset. The practice balances and harmonies the prana, chi or life force in the environment it is performed in. I have heard that it is effective for up to 1 kilometer in radius and 18kms up into the atmosphere. I don't know if the specifics are correct but it is what I heard. This is something so healing. Such a beautiful practice to gift your environment and community at large.

My trip to Byrock came about after I read a story about a woman who was giving free parcels of land. I called her up about the offer and she said I could come up to stay to see how I liked the place. At that time, they were in a severe drought.

At the same time, I also talked with other Agni Hotris (people who perform Agni Hotra) about them coming with me to Byrock. One of them then asked me if I was setting myself up for solitary confinement. I had no idea that that is pretty much what I would be doing.

However, all the people who were going to come with backed out before the trip, so I went alone. I caught the train from Southern Cross to Sydney, stayed at my aunt and uncle's place in Waverley overnight, and then caught the bus to Bourke the next day.

When I arrived, the son of the woman giving the land away. Picked me up and dropped me at the property. All I had with me was tea, but he told me that there was some food left for me. Fried rice and sausages. I said thank you but never actually ate it. I fasted for the first three days and just had chai there. There was an axe so I would go out during the day to chop wood, and make fires to make chai tea. Chopping wood and carrying water. Performing Agni Hotra at sunrise, then a tryambakam fire at 9am, vyaruhuti fire at 3 pm, Agni Hotra again at sunset and tryambakam at 9pm. The first few fires I did were very frustrating because all these insects would fly en masse into the fire. After trying a couple more times, I realized that this was part of the purification, so I simply accepted it.

On the third day, I slept in really late because I was very upset that I missed performing of three of the fires. Then again I realized that I am performing healing fires. So my sleep was my own healing.

This was part of my healing. I was in the middle of lighting the fire on the 5th day when it happened.

It rained.

There were only small drops, but it rained.

A year later, a male friend of mine and I travelled together to Bourke to attend the Yamma Festival, an indigenous festival. On the way to the festival, we also met another woman on the train who was also traveling there. We instantly became friends. We travelled and camped together by the river.

We were camping near a tree, and near us was a circle of bricks in which a fire can be lit. I would take small branches out from around the tree and put them in the fire and find the bricks and as I found them return them to the circle.

Throughout the entire festival, the elders looked after me and told me to make sure my male friend would escort me to the ladies. To make sure I wasn't attacked by any of the young boys. Some of them would actually throw things at me. One indigenous man called me the rain bringer. I knew he must have seen me in Byrock in the year earlier when I stayed there. Performing the healing fires.

At night, people would come at our campsite to sit around and sing. While my friend would play guitar by the fireplace. Everyone would play music and sing. In the day they had a damper making competition. Which was great fun. My Johnny Cake (damper) was the shape of a love heart. I didn't get any place and I was happy for the winners as theirs was magnificent. The ladies taught me the women's dancing. The movements demonstrate the gathering of berries. Looking for the berries. Then picking up the berries. Placing them in your basket. Then more looking. I loved this dancing.

On the last day if the festival, the elders gave me permission to perform Agni Hotra by the river. Afterward, we caught the bus back to Sydney and then the train home to Melbourne.

Another occasion, I stayed at a retreat with **Amma mataamritanandamayi.**

A woman also known as the hugging mother as she has traveled the world. Offering darshan and hugging soo many people.

The retreat was in Kyneton. I was camping by the lake rather than staying in a cabin. I slept inside a tent at the lakeside the whole time.

For each day of the retreat, we were required to do a half an hour of seva, which means selfless service. So, on the first day I did half an hour of food preparation, which involved chopping salad and vegetables in the food hall. Then I went into the main hall for darshan. I joined the long line of people kneeling on the floor while moving up the darshan line to receive darshan from Amma. Everyone was chanting *om nama shivaya*, Om Lokah Namasta Sukhino Bhavantu.

As I received my hug and lollies and rose petals from Amma on the first day. She whispered what sounded like hanuman, as she hugged me. I felt a brief Shakti pat (spiritual awakening). That evening, whilst I was sleeping in my tent. I again dreamt of receiving another darshan from Amma and feeling in a state of bliss. Shakti Pat all over again.

During the retreat, I befriended a mother and a young girl who were also camping beside me by the lake. The daughter wanted me to go canoeing around the lake with her. I was happy to oblige, and then it was time for Agni Hotra.

As I lit my fire, a man yelled at me from across the lake. However, I carried on knowing that by the time he reached me. After walking around the lake. That I would have finished my evening Agni Hotra. It did, just before he appeared before me and explained that it was a total fire ban.I had completed my Agni Hotra. I told him that I was performing a ritual to harmonize the prana and healing the atmosphere.

He apologized to me and also thanked me, and left. After that, I went back to the main hall for another Darshan with Amma. Once again, I experienced a Shakti pat when it was my turn to receive a hug and flowers from Amma. That night, I went back to my tent to sleep, and took the bus home by next morning.

On another journey on Australia Day, I traveled to the

aboriginal embassy tent. I initially met resistance from my mother, who worried that there might be trouble where I am going. I told her not to worry, that things will be fine, and traveled to Canberra by plane.

I arrived in the evening with only my carry-on luggage, my backpack, tent and a jembe hand drum. As soon as I got out from the airport, I took a taxi to the embassy tent. It was dark, but they had a chai tent. A young indigenous girl was singing, while videos of indigenous people throughout history played on a big screen.

I spent my first evening talking to people in the chai tent. The atmosphere was amazing! I couldn't be bothered putting my tent up. I just slept on the floor of the chai tent in my sleeping bag. The next day I got my period, with the accompanying menstrual cramps and pain. One of the older indigenous women, who was blind, was asking: "Is that a little white girl?" Someone told her yes. I once again spent all my time in the chai tent, but one man approached me and said he had pitched up my tent for me, which I was very grateful for. I slept in there that night.

The next afternoon, I got ready to leave. I packed my tent and started walking walking but one of the guys drove up to me in his van and told me that I had to come back for the smoking ceremony. So, I jumped in the van and went back with him. We all stood in a circle as they prayed. They lit the eucalyptus on fire and smudged us all with it. I felt so blessed to be a part of their sacred ceremony. The guy with the van then offered to drive me to the airport, which I accepted.

It was raining when we got to the airport, and my flight was delayed by thirty minutes. I felt disappointed. I could spent thirty minutes more at the original embassy tent.

I was twenty-seven the first time I was hospitalized for mental illness.

It so happened that my mother worked for a psychiatrist, so she called the cat team and they admitted me to the Royal Park Epic hospital. I had been honest and open about my clairaudience which to them is auditory hallucinations. So they locked me in a room with a seat and a window from which they would observe me.

My initial reaction to being institutionalized was anger. Every time they'd try to approach me, I would slam the door close on their faces and yell at them to go away.

It turns out that this was to be an experience and lesson about acceptance. I somehow lost track of time, but I felt that there was no use fighting my reality. I let go of my anger and resentment, and, once I did so, I gradually accepted my predicament.

As if on cue, the staff came in and told me that I would be released. Before that happened, I had several therapy sessions with the resident doctor. I told them that it was after I stopped using party drugs that I started experiencing the clairaudience.

One year later, I travelled to Perth and it was there that I met the astrologer who told me that my chart has four planets in the constellation of Pisces. These planets had activated, and that was the reason behind my abilities.

Also around this time, I was once in a spiritual bookstore and one general book. I saw had a picture of a shaman. However, next to the picture, it said a shaman in a transcendental state is what a western psychiatrist would describe as a schizophrenic.

Since my first hospitalization, I have been admitted another nine times, but my time of freedom has been spent traveling and growing spiritually: learning and studying all I can about tarot, palmistry, magic, spiritual healing as well as self-development and manifestation techniques.

At the same time, I pursue a habit of morning meditation and writing entries in my gratitude journal in the evening. I make it a point to be grateful for three- five events in each single day, that I am grateful for. I end the day with a candle meditation session, in which I would gaze at the flame for a few minutes before sleeping.

By the way, as I was heading back from Byrock aboard a train, I made the acquaintance of an elderly indigenous man who I also crossed paths with again at Yamma Festival in Bourke. He had performed a special smoking ceremony for me and my two friends, as he had already finished the sacred ceremony when we arrived.

Here's another example that I would like to highlight. While I was working at Telstra, we were told to put pictures of the places we wanted to go in the wall. For my part, I put in pictures of Thailand, Singapore and Indonesia.

I'm a firm believer. That it was through having this visua aid that would lead me on to later down the track be traveling to all these places. Thailand, Singapore and Indonesia.

It was incredible!

The islands were paradise: white, sandy beaches and beautiful blue waters. Beautiful sunny climate all around! We even traveled to Mt Agung. A volcanic mountain in bali. A lot of the other people. I was traveling with rode to the top of the volcano. Early in the morning, I was tired so I decided to sleep in. When I awoke I greatly appreciated the view of the mountain.

One night, I had the pleasure of viewing Prambanan Temple. Along with the light of the Full Moon! We were lucky enough to see a performance of the amazing Ramayana Ballet, under the light of the Full Moon and the Prambanan Temple in sight. The experience itself was beautiful and spectacular on its own!

When I arrived in Bangkok. On my second day in Thailand. I decided that the first thing I would do was visit the Waat Bang Praa Temple. Which is world renowned for its tattoos given by Buddhist monks. I was informed. I had to take took with me offerings of flowers, incense and cigarettes for these monks. Therefore I did just that and presented the monk who would tattoo me with my offerings.

The tattooing process was interesting. As the Buddhist monks can't touch women, two men held my arms on both of my shoulders.

While the monk used a bamboo stick to apply the tattoo to the top on my back where the neck meets the spine. The process was both pleasurable and painful! I didn't get to witness any Buddhist ceremony, however, as there was none at that time.

The next day, I paid a war site a visit, then had a cruise down the river by lunch time. Next, I went to the Tiger Temple where I was able to play with tiger cubs, and patted a huge tiger who was surprisingly docile. I suspected that they used drugs to tame the tigers, and that was exposed sometime later.

I also went to the popular island of Koh Phangan. One day I decided to go for a masssage. After my massage was finished. I met a lady and her partner. The lady owned the massage place and her partner had a Thai tattoo on his arm. I commented to him about his tattoo while having a cup of coffee with them both. I found out that he also received the tattoo from a Buddhist Monk. Who also gave him a ceremony for blessing and protection once he had completed the tattoo.

I told him of my experience at Waat Bang Praa. The man offered to help me book a visit to where he got his tattoo so I could get a tattoo and protection blessing ceremony afterwards as well.

I was thrilled and said yes right away. So, as soon as we finished our coffee, he and I rode to the tattoo temple on his motorcycle, where he secured an appointment for me.

He drove me back to my hotel on his motorbike, and gave my appointment card to the manager of my hotel. So that he could arrange someone to drive me to the tattoo parlour the next day.
With everything arranged, I slept well and woke up feeling excited for my trip to the tattoo parlor. Once there, I chose for my tattoo the symbols and blessings for good love, good family, good prosperity, peace and protection.

I was surprised that the tattoo artist had tattooed his entire body with the story of Buddha's life. I found him so attractive. He had

a lovely nature. After he gave me my tattoo, he lit incense, performed some prayers and performed my protection blessing ceremony. I loved it!
The experience was wonderful! Once again, the process of receiving the tattoo was a combination or both pleasure and pain but it was worth it!

After the ceremony, the man who was driving me. Delivered me back to my hotel. Let me tell about my accommodation here. I had chosen to stay in a bungalow that was so close to the beach, that I woke up seeing white sand and the clear blue waters of the Bay of Andaman ahead.

Indeed, Koh Pha Ngan is such a magical place!

While in Koh Pha Ngan, I also visited a place called the Amsterdam Bar. It is a rooftop bar, offering panoramic views of the beachscape all around it. We had the advantage of enjoying this view while dining and drinking by the balcony.

After Thailand, I went to Malaysia, where I had the extraordinary experience of my first encounter with a monitor lizard outside the hotel. At first, I freaked out because I thought it was a crocodile, but I was relieved when I found out what it really was. I still didn't go near it as I didn't want to disturb it.

In Penang, I bought a pair of Chinese bound shoes, but sold them later on. As I couldn't bear the image in my mind of how much of a torture it would have been to wear them!

Of course, while I was in Malaysia, I had to visit the popular Petronas Towers. We arrived in the late afternoon when the sun was still shining. But it was after sunset that we saw how beautiful the Towers really were! The view in the evening was something so spectacular.

After Malaysia, I had one day in Singapore. I visited Raffles Hotel, where I was amazed by all the peanut shells on the floor. I ordered a Singapore sling and I thought it tasted delicious!

I also went to visit Jurong Bird Park, which was home to 400 species of birds and 4,500 individuals of different colors and appearances! I'm actually scared of birds, and kept my distance from the avians during my visit but the sight of them was enough to amaze me!

After Singapore, we went to Indonesia. We stayed overnight in the capital, Jakarta, and travelled the next morning for Yogyakarta. Upon arriving, we immediately visited the Borobudur Temple just in time for sunrise. This temple is the largest Buddhist Temple in the world, and is a UNESCO World Heritage Site. It is surrounded by lush greenery and overlooks the distant Mount Merapi.

The next day I visited the Prambanan Temple, a 9th century Hindu temple dedicated to the Trimurti, the expression of God as the creator (Brahma), the preserver (Vishnu) and the Destroyer (Shiva). The temple compound is located approximately 17kms north east of Yogyakarta, right on the boundary with Central Java and Yogyakarta. That evening the others in the tour group decided on staying to enjoy the Ramayana ballet in the outdoor theatre beside Prambanan Temple.

I initially decided not to stay but changed my mind at the last minute. It's a good thing I did, because the Ballet performed under the light of a blue Full Moon.

The Ramayana is an ancient Sanskrit epic following Prince Rama's quest to rescue his wife Sita from Ravana with the help of an army of monkeys. The epic is believed to be written by the sage Valmiki and dated around 7600 B.C. I was so happy that I had decided at the last minute to watch the ballet!

When I returned to the hotel, the movie The Matrix was on TV. I decided to watch the film, I also was remembering I had a premonitory dream about this scenario happening in the past.

In fact, I have had many premonitory dreams of things that would occur in the future. These experiences made me decide on the name of my business, Psychic Dreaming.

After Yogyakarta, I travelled onwards to Ubud, where you can see lush fields and rice paddies. I basically pampered myself during my stay here. I enjoyed the services of day spas, having luxurious baths with essential oils, getting massages, and sampling the local food in the cafes and restaurants.

I also visited the Monkey Temple, which I had already gone to during my first time here. That time, I was traveling to Bali with three companions.

Ubud is a very lovely place, and coming back here for the second time was certainly worth it. It was a real treat, so to speak.

I returned home with many wonderful memories after three months of traveling. I will never understand. Why my father told me not to go overseas. In the time before he passed away he was always telling me he was dying and at the same time all I wanted was to enjoy whatever time I had left with him as I was always a daddy's girl.

Whenever he said that he was dying I would tell him this: "Dad. You're into Buddhism, (which he was in his later life). You know we are all dying from the day we are born, so don't give me this shit."

During his very last few days, he kept calling me on the phone each day. On the third day before his passing he was quoting Shakyumani Buddha to me. I'm not sure if I can recall it precisely, but it is something like this: "What have I taught, I have not taught that the body and soul are the same. I have not taught that the body and soul are separate. I have not taught that the soul does not exist after death. I have not taught that the soul does not exist after death. I have not taught that the soul is infinite. I have not taught that the soul is finite, and why have I not taught all these things. Because all these things are useless. They do not lead to the cessation of passion, peace, the holy life or nirvana, and what have I taught? I have taught that suffering exists, suffering has an origin and suffering has an ending. And why have I taught this? It's because this leads to the cessation of passion, peace, the holy life and nirvana."

After he recited this to me over the phone - he was in Queensland, and I was in Melbourne - at the time. So I asked him if he could send me a copy of this quote. The next day my father called me again telling me he had sent me a copy of the Buddha quote.

The day following that, I felt an inexplicable feeling of sadness while waiting tables at a diner in Brighton Breach. I couldn't understand at that time what I was feeling so down. So I went to the beach and sat down. This is something that I've never done before while working in the area.

The weather was overcast, and it rained while I was sitting on the beach, feeling sad and feeling puzzled why I was feeling this way. However, I saw a silver lining in the clouds while it rained.

I started recalling some lines from Desiderata, which my Dad had placed on back of the toilet door. So everyone could read it while using the toilet. Thinking the world really is beautiful.

I felt slightly better as it rained, although a heavy feeling of sadness still lingered. I only found out why when I returned home that day. That my father had passed away.

I received a phone call from a woman, who apologized for being the bearer of bad news, and she was asking me if I could go to my brother. I explained to her that he was in Queensland and I was in Victoria. She then proceeded to tell me to that my dad had passed away. As soon as she spoke those words. I cried, the floodgates of emotion opened. I cried myself to sleep the whole night.

I immediately flew to Queensland the next day to meet my other family and attend my dad's funeral and wake.

There was also that time in my earlier years when I had

dreamed about one of my friends getting killed in an accident while driving drunk. When one of my female friends told me that one of our friends, Roger, died from an accident, I told her about my dream, but I never thought it would be him.

Sometime after this, I went to see a medium, who summoned his spirit and communicate with me. He told me he had always loved me and that I should not be rebellious and try to fight the system.

I first became friends with Roger in first grade, when the boys would tease me for having big lips. He would come over stand in front of them, hold up his fist, and say to them: "You will have a big lip too if you keep that up!"

Years later, when my parents separated, my dad was living with his new girlfriend in the house next door to Roger's. Those days, I would hang out with Roger and his girlfriend, who was also a friend of mine.

I myself had a relationship in later years, or I thought I did. I was 27, and I was hospitalized for the first time. We were involved for a couple of years, until he called me to inform me that he had gotten another woman pregnant. The pain I felt that time was like a bullet that went through my heart.

Despite that, we continued to stay in touch, but it was never the same. I felt betrayed and didn't want to get back involved with him again. Years later he committed suicide. I was so sad, and decided to attend his funeral. Sometime after his funeral, a psychic I was in touch with told me his spirit hadn't properly crossed over because of regrets with regards to our relationship. I was advised to perform a love and forgiveness ritual to help him pass over, which I did.

My 33rd year in life was a big one, even though my dad passed away when I was that age. I became part of a program through my job network provider, which I thought was meant to improve your resume and interview techniques. It was really just to force me into working for a company that was engaged in debt collecting, which personally I would rather kill myself than do.

Before the program started, I had another dream. I was in India and I met a Guru walking down a street. Then, whilst doing the program the trainer was showing us the secret, all about the law of attraction. So, for the five days of the program, I had decided I wanted to go India. So each day I was affirming in my mind "I'm going to India, I'm going to India" even though I knew I didn't have the money for it. I just believed it would happen. On a Thursday, the trainer told me they wanted me to work for this debt collecting company.

On the Friday I would be interviewed for the position which I didn't want, the interviewer kept asking about, how I hadn't stuck to any one job for a long time. I just keep saying to him that I have been successful with every position I had ever held. It was awful after leaving there!

Afterward, I received a phone call from an acquaintance of mine who asked me to meet her by the Yarra. When we met, she asked me what was happening in my life. I told her about the program and the interview and that they wanted me to do a job debt collecting, which I didn't want to do. I also told her I want to go to India.

She said she could arrange for me to go to India, get a guru, and get married, instead of trying to bring an Indian man into the country. I said to her if I had to choose between becoming a debt collector or going to India to get a guru and get married, as far as I was concerned, it was a no brainer, I would rather go to India, get a guru and marry. So, I called the job agency and told them I was going to India. They were asking me who bought my ticket, I told them it's none of their business.

My ticket to India was bought and paid for and I had a guru. I was so excited, I spoke to my guru over the phone and had a really good feeling about him. He told me I would be welcome and everything would be fine.

I immediately flew to Mumbai, where my guru had told me one

of his Shishirs (disciple of a guru) would pick me up at the airport. After picking me up, the disciple drove to a restaurant and had an Indian vegetarian curry. He then took me by bus to Ahmedabad, where my guru's apartment was. The bus trip was very long, and there were many stops along the way for chai, snacks and toilet breaks. My guru had another shishir living with him in his apartment named Happy.

A year before flying to India, I had a dream of being in an apartment with two men speaking a foreign language. That time, I just woke up and remember thinking as if that is going to happen. In my time staying with my guru, it did happen exactly as in my dream. I realized it was another of my premonitory dreams, and I laughed in glee when it came true and as I remembered my reaction upon waking up that day.

My guru asked me why I was laughing so I told him about my dream and how I never thought it would actually happen. On another occasion, I told my guru about how I had met him in my dream before we were even in contact. He admitted to me that he had sent his energy out to me, and I was destined to be his shishir.

The very first day I spent with him and with two other shishirs, he taught us deep breathing techniques. He also made us drink boiled salt water and throw it up. He said that this is what we should do if we were ever poisoned by anyone.

Every day, he insisted I do puja, which I did. I was given a special mantra to repeat which I was not to tell anyone. I was also given my Hindu guru name, which is Maha Chaitanya Rudra, but everyone just called me Rudra. I also practiced Agni hotra which I love so much more than performing puja. I also spent time staying with my guru's family in Dhandhukka, with his wife and daughter and son. I loved staying there, there was so many animals and every time I would perform Agni hotra the animals loved it and enjoyed the energy.

There was also another Australian shishir, whose name was

Christopher. One day he and I went to guru in the morning. He had already spoken to guru on the phone earlier as well and we had to go to the school as they were delivering the furniture by truck. Guru told us to go there and he said good luck. So we walked over to the school, the truck arrived with all the desks and chairs and furniture, but only one man was unloading it. So I started helping, telling the other men to help although they didn't understand English and just laughed at me. So Chris and I carried the desks and chairs into the
school together with that one man. Soon after, the children started helping us. We managed to unload the whole truck, but it took hours. I felt so proud afterwards and Chris was saying now he understood why guru had said good luck.

In another day, Chris and I had to meet some other special guru. We sat in front of him and he was saying something like what you think is freedom is not true freedom. And what you think is not freedom is true freedom. It really struck something in me about the times. I had been incarcerated in the hospitals because at times I would just refuse to speak to the doctors. Listening to this guru, I felt there was truth in what he was saying.

I met my husband on just a few occasions before we had our wedding ceremony. Our wedding day was a huge celebration with hundreds of people. Most of whom, I didn't know except my husband's family. The woman dressed me twice in two different beautiful saris and jewelry. Although the saris are beautiful, I found them so uncomfortable.

We were married through a Hindu ceremony with a Bupu (Hindu Priest), and there was a havand, fire ceremony. There were gerberas everywhere. The gerbera is one of my favorite flowers. After the ceremony, there was a huge feast where vegetarian curry, papadums and gulab Jamon for dessert were served. I was never intimate with my husband as he didn't speak English and I didn't speak Gujurati.

We applied at the Australian embassy in New Delhi but his

application was rejected. I loved New Delhi. It was full of colours, and market stalls. One day, as I walking down one of the streets, a man invited me into his store for chai. He also showed me photos of his houseboat, that he took people on tours on.

On our way to New Delhi, guru and I were being driven by Raj in his car. He stopped by the roadside to see this elderly man. The man was Jain. It was the strangest experience as soon as they stopped the car. I got out and felt an overwhelming urge to hug him straight away. As I felt as if I knew him. Guru and Raj got out and guru was translating what was saying as we were hugging, and he was saying, "I had been a peace lover from way back and he remembered me" Then they spoke and before I knew it we were leaving again.

As we were leaving, I asked Guru if we would see him again. Guru said he had invited us back for chai the next day. I knew we wouldn't see him again and we didn't.

Raj loved me and said he called himself my Indian father. It turned out the man by the roadside was Raj's father. Guru told me in one of my past lives he and I were Jains.

Jainism is a religion in India. The main religious premises of Jainism are (AHIMSA) non-violence, Aparigraha (non-attachment), Anekantavada and ascetism. Jains take five main vows ahimsa (non-violence), satya (truth) asteya (not stealing), Brahmacharya (celibacy, chastity or sexual continence) and aprigrahgraha (non attachment).

Later on, I did have a dream that I was a Jain, confirming what guru told me on the night when we were traveling with Raj. Guru and I stayed at his house. At that time, the two dogs were fighting and Raj looked at me and said "neh shanti," which means "not peaceful." I understood and I laughed, as did he.

On our way back from Delhi to Amhedabad. We stopped at a small village town overnight. I met another Hindu priest and asked him, with Guru translating of course if I could perform Agni hotra with him in the morning. While he performed his puja, he agreed. So I gathered some cow dung that night, and slept early to be up for a sunrise agni hotra. When the sun rose, he performed puja while I performed agni hotra. I was in a deep meditative state, and it was wonderful. While in that trance, I received a message that I would achieve peace in my lifetime.

We returned to Guru's flat in Ahmedabad. There was also a German woman, another shishir, who stayed. She argued with me so much that I learned a valuable lesson. If someone doesn't appreciate your company, walk away and find other company instead that will appreciate you. So, in the morning, I would rise before she did and go down the street. I would sit at the chai stall with the Indian men who were so nice to me, and I was much happier. I would perform Puja and Agni Hotra. Those were wonderful days.

One day, Chris and I were staying once more in Guru's home in Dhandhukka. Guru found a beautiful white owl that was sick. We tried to nurse it back to health, but it died. I felt very sad while burying it, and I remembered my own pets in the past.

I once had a dog named Zany. Zany was a cross between and a Doberman and a ridgeback.

Now, Guru had a dog named Zoro, and he would sit with me while I performed the Agni Hotra. Guru also had another 10 dogs, together with 30 doves and pigeons. We had to feed and look after these, and, to my dismay, to share a room with them.

I fear birds greatly after watching Alfred Hitchcock's "The Birds" film at a young age. I admire their beauty, but I am happy to look at them from a distance only.

In addition to feeding the birds, I also help out in washing dishes and preparing food for everybody.

Guru also had four ducks, which the dogs slaughtered over time. There was also a cow at his property in Dhandhukka, which we

would milk every morning. Every day, I would have to walk across the paddock to get some dahi, while children would follow
me while yelling out my name. Cows and buffalos would also follow me around as well!

I thought, this must be what it's like to be famous!

One day Guru introduced me to four young girls and told me to teach them English. They were lovely girls and they learnt quite well. I started using books but then I realized it was British English and not things they would say. There was also a lot of text about meat, which they don't eat as they are vegetarian.

Until now, I'm still in touch with one of the four girls, who also teaches English now. She proudly told me once that all of her students got high marks in English!

After their lessons in the afternoon we would sit on the cots outside and just talk. I visited many temples prayed constantly as well as performed puja and agni hotra. When I would perform agni hotra, Zorro would be sitting beside me and will not leave my side until the fire was finished. Guru's shishirs would be feeding the dogs and calling Zorro for his dinner, but he would never get up to go till after the fire was complete. If any pups come near the fire, he would bark them away.

One day, Guru taught me a meditation that sends healing to people. It was something like this: envision the person who is in need of healing. See them in a temple and lay them down on a bed. I would always envision a rose quartz bed for them to lay on, and then call in their angels and ascended masters to perform healing on them. I should also say a prayer for their healing to be complete. See them stand and leave the temple fully healed.

This is something I would meditate and visualize daily, at one time a woman who was friends with guru, who looked after many dogs was very badly beaten and she had to have surgery. So I stayed in hospital for one week. Guru sent me to stay with her to give her reiki daily. She was very badly bruised so I also managed to get her some arnica cream and applied it on her bruises daily, aside from doing hands on reiki. Arnica cream helps clear up bruising.

By the end of the week she was much better and could return home. So I returned to Dhandukka, where I was staying. In his property, Guru had a small house with two rooms that he had hopes of developing into an ashram, which sadly never came to pass.

When he would speak of his dream, I knew somehow in my heart that it would not materialize and it never did. He would read my coffee grounds in my cup each morning. He told me things about my future. He also told me he would die young. He was only a couple of years older than me, and, as he said, he did pass away young.

I'm so grateful for all the time I had with him. He was the most popular person that I have ever known. Everyone would come and wait in line to see him for advice or guidance. At the same time, his phone of course would not stop ringing off the hook.

One day, a young man came walking up the front towards the house. I assumed he was coming to see guru to my surprise. He had come to meet me and said that he wanted to take me to meet his family as they had never seen a white person. He lived in a small village half an hour away. These days, I can no longer remember the exact name of the village. We went there by Chokura, which is a three wheeled bike, where you jump on the back tray to ride.

So, we journeyed to his town and, there, I found so many people and none of them had never seen a white person before. All of them wanted to touch me and stroked my arm. I was a little bit amazed that they hadn't seen a white person before!

After I had been in India for six months, I needed to renew my visa. So guru and his Shishir took me to Kathmandu in Nepal. While there, I had a brief romance. I had wanted to see the temple in Kathmandu called Pashupharti Nath, but I wasn't allowed in because he said I looked American. I told the guy there that I was Australian and had never set foot on US soil. I also said to him I can't believe I'm experiencing Nepalese racism. However, as I didn't have my passport to prove to him that I was Australian, I wasn't allowed in.

One day, while I was sitting in the reception area of the hotel, a man came in and asked me where I had been. I told him I was just here at the hotel and the internet café. He kindly offered to take me around and I asked if I could just introduce him to my guru first. He agreed and met Guru, who said I could go with him. He took me to a really amazing Buddhist temple with a large statue of Buddha and the golden wheel. I was told that, if I walk around it and make a wish, it will come true.

At the moment, he was telling me I could make my wish, I didn't know what to wish for so I decided to pray instead, and prayed and walked around the golden wheel. After that, I once again rode on the back of his bike to a wonderful Nepalese restaurant where we had delicious vegetarian dumplings. After the meal, he took me back to my hotel.

We were supposed to return to India the next day. However, there had been some violent protests. Bombs planted in buses destroyed the roadways, so a trip by land was out of the question. We decided to get tickets to a Buddha Air flight to the Nepal-India border instead.

We flew on board a small aircraft named Buddha airways. It was small, but comfortable. Moreover, the views I saw during the plane ride were incredible! We could see the snowy capped mountains of the Himalayas. A breathtaking and beautiful sight! I now wish I had taken photos, but I was much too awed and in love with views to have snapped any.

And, oh, I forgot to mention a couple of amazing experiences I had in lovina in Indonesia.

While on my way into town, I noticed a sign in front of a building with a picture of a palm and text saying "palmistry readings." I decided to go there one night. I had a bit of a challenge finding the place again, but one of the locals gave a lift there on the back of his bike.

The place was owned by a lovely Hindu woman. She told me I would marry in my early 40's. Right now, I'm 47 and still unmarried, but maybe it will happen sometime in my 40's. She told me my future husband will be handsome, successful, and not from the same country as me. In other words, he would be a foreigner to me.

The next day I woke early in the morning, around 4:30. I was excited, because I will be going out on a boat to be with the dolphins. It was a lovely sunny morning. There was also many other tourists, including Buddhist monks all taking photos of the dolphins swimming around and jumping and diving back in the water.

Now, getting back to India…

Everyone tells you about the shock when experiencing India for the first time. However, no one ever tells you about going home from the first time you travelled to India.

For myself, when that day came, I kept telling myself that I'm going back one day. I know it sounds strange because, at that time, I've only been in India for the first time, but I felt like I have lived there for a long time. It felt to me as though I was returning somewhere I had been before. I must have had a past life in India.

My first journey to India was only for two and a half months. When I returned home, I found it really hard to readjust to my life in Melbourne, Australia. I did return to India for a second time, but when I returned, I found it easy to settle back to life in the Land Down Under.

In my second journey to India, I visited a healer out in the country who told me that if I went back to my life in Australia, I'd become a slave. He also asked me if I wanted to be a slave.

I have always believed it is important to help people

numerologically. The number 33 is always associated with a master healer. Christ was a thirty-three, and died at 33 years old, but it also goes to a 6, which is all about selfless service. This is what I have spent my life doing - serving people in one way or another.

My Mayan calendar affirmation is. "I activate in order to enlighten, bonding life. I seal the universal fire with electric tone of service. I am guided by the power of flowering."

After returning to India from Nepal. I was back to where guru always hoped to establish an ashram. There was also a school next to it that guru's wife ran and in between the two buildings was a field where all the boys and men would play cricket, and where cows and buffalos would walk around the place as well.

The Bupu (Indian priest) of a nearby temple took a liking to me and one day invited me to spend the day with him at the temple. I arrived in the morning and we gathered items for praying in the temple then prayed with the large Shiva Lingam, washing it and offerings or flowers and fruit.

After praying, we moved to the garden, where there was as swing by the tree. Bupu would sit there, until afternoon, when we would prepare to pray again and followed by the Bhajans. These people play music and sing but I always found it strange that they don't want to dance.

After the Bhajans are finished, I would return by chokura, the tree wheeled bike, to Guru's home.

In other days I would do my washing and collecting items for Puja as well as visit temples around to pray. In the evening, I would prepare the vegetables for cooking. Guru and his Shishir would cook Guru's amazing all vegetarian recipes. These are so delicious!

I would also make chai from scratch with spices. Sometimes, I would go to Ahmedabad and stay with families that were friends or Guru's and would have to help with cooking as a reprieve from doing daily puja. I would also miss a few days of Agni Hotra, though, one day, a friend of Guru's that I was staying with took me to the Sai baba ashram where I found out that he was also friends with the Bupu.

As part of our praying preparations, we had to wash ourselves and wipe the floor of the temple clean. While I was doing this, I just wanted to cry and I couldn't understand why I was just overcome with emotion from the prayers.

After the prayers by the Bupu were complete, he gave us Prasad which I would distribute to anyone I crossed paths with until they were all gone.

One day, there was a big celebration at Guru's where Bupus from all over India and performed Havands for hours, with flowers, rice and glee as offerings.

Afterwards there was a big feast. I served food to everyone. I didn't really know what it was for or about but I enjoyed being with all the holy men and just prayed anyway and served. I also looked after the children and babies

I also once stayed with the family, friends of Guru's in Ahmedabad. One man, who was a journalist, kept saying to me I should write a story of all my love affairs. He kept saying that he thought everyone would want to read that, but I told him I'm not into romance writing. However, I felt a bit flattered that he thought my love life would be a successful and fascinating story. It wasn't something that I would have ever considered or occurred to me though.

I spent a lot of time with his wife's mother feeding the dogs and cooking. Now, dogs aren't treated well by most in India. They treat them terribly, even run them over. If ever I saw a dead dog on the road it would break my heart and I would feel sad as I have always loved dogs.

I couldn't get used to the fact that they mistreat dogs in India, and it just made me so sad.

Thankfully, on the other hand, I also knew people who were doing their best to look after them, as well as myself.

After my father passed away. I received a small inheritance. Afterward, I saw an advertisement in a spiritual magazine about a tour to go to wellington, New Zealand to have healing from John of God. He is a Brazilian miracle healer that I've heard about, and I decided I wanted to do the tour. So, I went ahead and booked myself for the tour.

I only wanted to book a stay at a backpackers' hotel when I visited the travel agent. However, they booked me in to a very good one. For this trip, I bought a couple of bottles of Johnny Walker Scotch whiskey. I thought I'll have a few drinks the night before I meet John of God, because it is said that you have to abstain from eating pork, drinking alcohol and having sex for about a month after receiving his blessing.

I arrived in Wellington early in the morning and dropped my things off of the backpackers' hotel. I decided to walk around the city and have breakfast and coffee. I could see why they called it the windy city, as it was really windy. I spent the day just looking around and slept early. The next day, I relocated to the other hotel and joined the tour group. We were given a bag of goodies and informed of our itinerary for John of God's healings.

On the first night in the new hotel, I dreamt of Maoris performing a welcome session for John of God, which, later I discovered, actually happened. The John of God healings were at a large hall that's a bit of a walk away from the hotel. We would be going to experience his healings on our second day there.

On the evening, I met a man whom I ended up drinking my scotch with, just talking and laughing he was telling me all about his family. Soon after I left and sat outside for a while, a little drunk I admit, I was recalling how my father loved Scotch and here I was having used his inheritance for this trip. I was sending my father love and thanking him and just remembering him.

There would be two types of healing you could receive from John of God. One was psychic surgery, which worked on your energy. The other one is spiritual surgery, which they said was like having an actual surgery. If you received spiritual surgery, you were told to have 24-hour bed rest and take it easy in the following days. All of these were captured by a film crew filming in the hall.

When I arrived, the hall was full of people waiting to receive healing from John of God. He was sitting on a chair, and there were pictures of guidelines of his healing spread throughout the hall. When my turn came, I was asked into a room where I was to sit and meditate whilst receiving the healing. After I had my time with John of God, I was told that I had the spiritual surgery so I returned to the hotel for my bed rest. I felt disappointed as I had hoped I would only have the psychic surgery and did not really want to have a lot of bed rest. I followed their advice nonetheless.

A lot of people there were saying I was lucky to have the spiritual surgery and they only had psychic surgery. That night, things got a little exciting as there was a small earthquake. Thankfully, it was only a very minor one, but some people were saying they felt it. For the rest of tour I needed rest and it actually felt like a bit of a cold.

In my last day in wellington I moved back to the backpackers again. I met some people there and ended up going out dancing for the night before catching the plane home in the morning. I had a really fun night with a young Englishman who shared my love of drums and bass. He drank, but I didn't as per instructions. We also danced and played pool all night, until it was time to go to sleep. I caught the shuttle from the backpackers at 5:30am to return to the airport and then home to Melbourne Australia.

Now, many years later, it has been discovered that John of God was sexually abusing or assaulting young girls, keeping them and selling the babies if they got pregnant. I was so shocked and horrified when I learnt this.

When I was told at 13 that I had the gift or intuition, and that, throughout my life, it would be a blessing and a curse at the time, I didn't understand. Now I do after being hospitalized 10 times for so called "mental illness."

In the shamanic view of things, mental illness signals the birth of a healer, which I was told I would be during another reading at a younger age.

The only time I ever ended up in hospital for harming myself was after my first hospitalization. I took an overdose of my pills, which landed me back in hospital, and eating charcoal to get back to normal.

The only reason I took that overdose was because of the trauma from my first admission. All admissions after that I would just spend my time chanting to keep in a state of peace.

With schizophrenia, there is a special receptivity to a flow of images and information which cannot be controlled when one is experiencing an episode. These images are not personally chosen and particularly when it comes with images that are scary and contradictory, the person goes into a frenzy. What is required is a shamanic sweep to clear the person's aura, and not hospitalization nor medication.

The shamanic approach is to work on aligning the energies so there isn't a blockage, and the person can become the healer they are meant to be. I had to find my own way through learning healing modalities. I started with Reiki in my twenties, gaining my Reiki master rank in my 30's and, ultimately, my grandmaster rank in my 40's.

Let me explain Reiki for a bit. Reiki level 1 teaches you hands-on Reiki, which means you need to be physically there with the recipient. As a Reiki master or grandmaster. You can send Reiki remotely to anyone anywhere in the world.

Now that I have my Reiki grandmasters, I perform sessions absently. I write down the intended recipient's full name, place my hand over it, and visualize sending all Reiki symbols to him or her. Whilst I am sending, I can feel whatever is going in the recipient's body. As part of the healing, I always send the person feedback regarding what I felt during the session. To date, with every session and feedback sent to each recipient, I have only ever received confirmation that what I felt during remote healing was correct.

Reiki has been around for a while now. It was first channelled by Dr. Mikao Usui in 1992. Since then, there have been many lineages worldwide. I also attained up to level 3 in the Melchizedek method. I have already learned levitation, which is a strange yet wonderful feeling.

Chapter 2

Kindness Matters

Bi-location is a skill in which is when you send your spirit somewhere else. Whilst still being conscious of the surroundings you are physically in. Once, when I was hospitalized, a friend of mine had invited me to a meditation for world peace. As I was in hospital, I was unable to physically attend. What I did was I sat chanting the "Padme Om" for the entire time that the meditation was ongoing. Afterwards, my friend called me and said during the meditation he saw my spirit there in the meditation with everyone. I had been bi- locating without even knowing it!

I have also learnt Theta healing and serenity vibrational healing. Throughout my life, learning about magic, spirituality and healing has been like a thirst in my life. I just want to learn more and more, although I haven't as yet advanced or learnt how to become a medium. As my Guru once told me, I have latent mediumship abilities but have left them undeveloped.

As I said earlier, my Guru passed away at a young age. Worse, my Guru and my grandma passed away just a week apart from each other. It was a harrowing time for me. I was so depressed after losing two people close to me in quick succession.

My grandma was in her 80's. She had a good life, but I knew I would miss her. On the other hand, my Guru was young. He was actually only a couple of years older than me. He knew he would pass at a young age and had told me this. I wasn't prepared for how tragic his passing would be. He was a smoker. One day, he was lighting his Bidi (Indian cigarette), on the gas cylinder, his flammable jacket caught fire, 75% of his body was burnt, and he was on life support for

a few days until he passed away. I can still remember the day I left India. He was hugging me and telling me this was my home and I was always welcome to return. Something told me I wouldn't and,
as we drove off, I knew this was the last time I would see him. It turns out that I was correct. Now, it's always baffled me as to why I knew it was the last time I would see him, but I didn't get that feeling the last time I saw my father. With my dad, I had no idea and I had thought I would see him again.

I received an inheritance from my grandma which allowed me travel to Thailand, Malaysia, Singapore, Indonesia, and, years later, to travel to Qatar for one month with my African boyfriend that I met over the internet.

He pre-arranged our accommodation with an Indian couple in their Villa, where we stayed the whole time as it is forbidden for us to be seen in public together under Sharia law. There are some African men staying in the complex with us as well.

One day, I was arriving home from shopping when the Indian man who owned the Villa met me at the gate and told me to tell my love not to come back until it was safe. It turned out that one of the other African men in the Villa had been caught by police and was being deported. The Indian owners feared that if my boyfriend and I were seen together, we would also be deported from Qatar.

So I called my love and told him to go to the shops, do some shopping, or have his dinner out until I called him to tell him it's safe to come home. After some hours, the man who owned the villa said he didn't think the police would return, so I called my love and told him it was safe for him to come home now.

During that month in Qatar, I visited the Souq Waqif, an old market with a mosque in the background with narrow alleys and shops selling spices, antiques and eateries. One of my friends wanted me to bring her back rose oil, which I found in one of the shops. I also rented a shisha and smoked strawberry tobacco while having a coffee. I also visited museums and art galleries and shopping centers.

However, our relationship ended not long after I went home to Australia. He had married an African woman from his home country. Just as I had a feeling would happen. It turns out that my intuition is, again, correct.

When I was in Malaysia, I met a man who looked at my hand and he predicted that, at 45, I would have my own business, which came true. I now spend time offering tarot readings professionally as well as distance reiki sessions with feedback sent afterwards. I also offer my tarot services for parties, where I offer 5 minute readings for large number of people.

In the past, I also acquired certificates. Four were in tourism as I did work in a travel agency briefly. Before that, I also attained a certificate in music. I had the opportunity to work with great musicians while being involved in various Work 4 The Dole programs. I was actually interested in pursuing a record, but the musicians I worked with were already committed to their own bands.

It was after attending a goals workshop that I decided to start my own business reading tarot and giving healings. A year ago, I attended a masterclass about living your dream life, and there was an exercise where we had to write out our dreams without thinking about any constraints like time, money or execution. My first dream was to write and publish the story of my life. Exactly one year later, I have manifested it! I have always been good at manifesting my dreams into reality, just through believing they would happen. Also I love to read about manifesting.

Also, a year ago, I had a coffee reading and the person who read my coffee predicted many things. One of them said that I would get a job working in a healing centre in the country, which has come true.

My dreams so often show me events that will happen like one

time I had a dream that one of my girlfriends who is living further up north would come to Melbourne for a holiday. I would get to see her then. She did come to Melbourne but I didn't get to see her. I also have an office job which I was dreaming about a few weeks ago. The dream also showed one of my supervisors. Since having the dream, I discovered that that particular supervisor will be leaving and the office will be moving. That explained my dream.

When I was growing up as a kid, I attended dance lessons. I used to love dancing; it was often a way for me relieve any frustrations I was feeling. I started the dance classes at age 5 and continued up until I was about 15. I still continued to dance for years after. I was in my early 20's when I got an interview for a dance school Academy. The night before the interview I had danced all night in a club. At the interview I had to demonstrate the foxtrot and have everyone else follow my steps. Afterwards I went into the interview room, where the interviewer told me I didn't get the job and that I needed to dance more.

Chapter 3

Take It Slow

They definitely must have thought I was crazy as I left there laughing hysterically. I was thinking that, if I danced more, I would die!

As a teenager, I once landed the role of the cat in a musical production of Puss in Boots. The production would perform for kids during school holidays in shopping centres around Brisbane, and The Gold Coat. I had a lot of fun in these productions.

I was always better at dancing and singing than acting though.

In the nine months. I spent staying at my Guru's place in Dhanhukka, for many a night I shared a room with thirty doves and pigeons which was really unnerving for me. One time, Guru asked me to take a dove out of its cage.

I said, "No way!"

He said, "Don't you want to get rid of that fear?"

I said, "No, thanks, I'm okay with it."

Now, fast forward to 2019.

I have just returned from the Christmas holidays with my family in New South Wales. My uncle has always said I was a jetsetter from the day of my birth.

I was born at Tamworth base hospital. I was resuscitated at birth then flown by air ambulance to a Sydney hospital and put in a humidity crib. The doctors thought I may have brain damage.

However, the only thing that was wrong with me was that I was severely dehydrated as no one had given me anything to have to drink.

My time with the family for Christmas was great but went too quickly. One morning while I was there, I performed Agni Hotra. It was a lovely fire, and, as I was performing the ritual, he birds were coming around to be in the energy. Birds and animals love the energy and are always drawn to it every time I perform.

I have also been chanting mantras like the Lakshmi mantra, which is for abundance and goes this way: "OMHRIM KRIM SHRIM MAHA LAKSHMMI Namaha." I chanted the BIJA MANTRA, which is for healing, and goes like: "Lam, Vam, Ram, Yam, Ham, Aum." It also balances and energizes the physical, emotional and energy bodies.

As mentioned earlier, I also write a gratitude journal daily. Yesterday was the summer solstice, so I performed a spell for clarity before starting. I did a clearing by ringing my bell throughout the house, which you can do to clear away any negative energy.

After performing the spell, I did some divination with my pendulum and finished off with the chanting 108 times of "Om lokah namaste sukhino Bhavantu," which means may all sentient beings be well and happy.

Lately I have been chanting that, and I can't believe it is already Christmas 2019! I feel so blessed and grateful for all the wonderful connections. I have family and friends around the world. I have been giving and receiving gifts and I am so thankful for my life. Today I received my spell box for next month's January spell and it is for a resolution.

So, for me, I will resolve to finish writing this book. I just won another prize, a number of crystals which I will put to good use in February when I begin holding crystal workshops.

My life has been a real juxtaposition. At times when I am serving clients, be it at a tarot party, reading, or Reiki healing, I am treated respectfully by all my clients. Then, there is the other end of the Scale: the Doctors, Psychiatrists and case workers. I can feel that they look down at me as they have labeled me insane. I feel what is truly insane is the fact that in Australia we are supposed to be living in a democracy yet in reality it has become a kleptocracy.

At this moment in Australia, bushfires are raging all over. It is heartbreaking. War is advertised as something glamorous when reality it is horrific. The Government implements forced Psychiatry so that big Pharma profits. They don't want people to truly heal as there is no money in that for them. We are their experiments.

Meanwhile, we all have our politicians, who are profiting from raping the earth. Coal is a finite resource and will run out. It also makes people ill. It should be left in the ground. There is so much logging is going on that species are dying out from loss of habitat.

There are still people hunting our whales and dolphins, the most beautiful creatures of the sea. Yet, in the midst of these atrocities, there are people (like myself) praying for peace, fighting for the environment and the animals.

This world is insane. I can only hope and pray that one day peace will prevail and the people practice Agni Hotra to keep the peace and heal. In the face of these tragic fires, it is heartening to see people coming together to assist those in need as well as the surviving animals. So many people are donating items needed to assist in the care of the wildlife, and the people stuck in evacuation shelters. There are those who pitch in money for those in need as well.

Sadly lives have been lost and most of our wildlife and nature but the positive is that people are rallying together to assist those in need and the animals that have survived. Tonight is a full moon eclipse. I did a wonderful spell for resolution, and the energy was incredible. I did a visualization of my dreams and goals being fully realized in my life. It felt like such a powerful and potent spell.

Speaking of magic - I thought I would include and share the magical correspondences for the days of the week. They are as follows:

- · Sunday: The sun God, Sol, representing agriculture, beauty, hope, victory, self-expression and creativity. Plant or harvest something new (not just material crops, but metaphysical ones as well.) Create something from nothing and prepare to win at everything.
- · Monday: Goddess moon, Mani's day. This is a good time to focus on working. Related to childbearing and family life, purity and virginity, healing, wisdom and intuition do a little bit of self-exploration and working on your intuition, celebrating Birth and Life.

Chapter 4

Think well feel well

- Tuesday: Mars, God of war, Tyr's day. A day for magical workings connected to protection and initiation. Use Tuesday to assert yourself, make a mark and or stake your claim!
- Wednesday: Mercury, ODIN, The Raven God. Business and job-related issues, communication, loss and debt, traveling and journeys are all tied in to Wednesday. This is a good day to open up the lines of communication. Go to someplace new or return to visit a favorite place.
- Thursday: Jupiter, Thor, God of Strength and storms. This is a day for honor, family loyalty, as well as harvesting, success and prosperity. Do spell work for abundance, declare your allegiance and embrace prosperity.

Chapter 5

Feed your soul

- Friday: Venus, Hera, Goddess of marriage, love and beauty are associated with Friday. A good day to do spell work associated with family life, fertility sexuality, harmony friendship, growth and love.
- Saturday: Saturn, god of wealth and time. For magical workings focus on agriculture and creativity, fortune and hope, protection and banishment of negativity. Put up a barrier to keep out the unwelcome, eliminate the things that make you miserable, wash your hands of anything other than your hopes, dreams and goals. This morning I joined in a zoom call where people from all over the world prayed, meditated and danced to aboriginal music with the intention of bringing the rains to the fire affected areas of Australia. It was so heartening that there were so many people involved in collective prayers, meditations, dances, drumming and singing. It worked the rains came and put out 31 fires. Yay!

Whilst I was living in India, I read many amazing books. I read an autobiography or a Paramahansa Yogananda, as well as the messenger of the Sacred Fire by Parvati Rosen-Bizberg.

Whilst I was reading these books, I was really hoping and praying that one day it would be my destiny to meet the amazing man Shree Vasant Paranjpe. However, one day, I learned that he had died. I cried so many tears that day. I was heartbroken that I will not get to meet him.

However, Shree Vasant Paranjpe appeared to me in a dream and talked to me about consciousness and ascension. I awoke from the dream feeling revitalized and in a state of bliss.

As I have said earlier, my Guru told me I had latent mediumship abilities. I experience many occasions where mental telepathy makes me aware that someone is going to call when I think of them, or they think of me and I call them. We all experience mental telepathic connections with one another. After attending workshop on Agni Hotra, I learnt something important - the Ghee that is used as the offering along with the full grains of organic brown rice must only be yellow ghee. It should never be white or clear, or else it has aged. You should not use aged ghee. It must be strictly fresh. Also, when lighting it, it is preferable to light from an oil lamp. In some cases, matches will do, but never an oil lighter.

The corners or your copper pot should be facing north, south, east, west, I was also reminded of the fact that Agni Hotra in reality is not a ritual it is actually a super seance that cleanses 7 generations. When Agni Hotra is performed, there is an influx of prana that comes from the Sun.

Chapter 6

Put it into words

Agni Hotra purifies seven levels of consciousness and brings prana to an area approximately 1 kilometre in radius, and 16 kilometres up into the atmosphere.

There have been so many people who have been recovered from various illnesses when they have adopted a daily practice of Agni Hotra into their lives. There are people all over the world who use Agni Hotra for the health and well-being of crops that they are growing also.

One night when I was living in the mansion in Caulfield I came home in the evening and opened one of our three fridges and pulled out a huge green vegetable. I didn't know what it was until one of the housemates told me it was a cucumber out of our garden. Its size and health must have been due to me spreading the Agni Hotra ashes on the garden.

It was so large that one slice would cover a whole loaf of bread. I thought I might also go over the witches' calendar, which is known as the spinning wheel or the observation of the Sabbats. The Sabbats are the traditional Wiccan holy days that symbolize birth, growth, death and rebirth. Four Sabbats fall on the equinoxes and solstices (yule 21st December-Summer solstice, Ostara, 21st March autumn equinox, Litha 21st June winters solstice, Mabon, 21st Sep. Spring equinox), while the remaining fall at the midway points Imboic, Beltane, Lammas and Samhain. Celebrating these days with rituals and offerings is referred to as the turning of the wheel. Each of these holy days gives us the opportunity to celebrate Nature and the passing of time.

Yesterday was the 1 February, Lammas so I performed a spell for a romance to mend, forgive and heal from previous failed relationships and be hopeful to find a healthy, happy relationship in future. At the beginning of this week, there was a full super moon. I performed my spell for grounding, which I feel is helping me immensely as I only have one earth sign in my astrological chart. Thus, grounding is always something I need.

I also created a crystal grid for abundance. I already feel so abundant. I have somewhere to live, family, friends and many wonderful treasures in my life; I am so blessed and grateful. Gratitude is something I practice daily. I always keep a gratitude, Journal although this year. I won a gratitude diary for 2020, so I am writing in its daily.

I once wrote a gratitude list of 100 things I have in my life. I also recently had to ask my friends a series of questions about myself. One of the questions was" "What would you criticize about me?"

One of my friends said that she doesn't don't know enough about how to manifest. I said that keeping gratitude helps you manifest because you are focusing on the appreciation and feeling good really does help you manifest what you want.

It's now March 2022 and the global pandemic Covid-19 is happening. I always intuitively knew there would come a time when supermarket shelves would be emptied, and we would have martial law, that time is now. All my work in the new age store and tarot party work has come to a halt.

Despite that, I'm grateful for my phone and online readings. I have been spending my time doing daily morning meditations, writing daily gratitude, chanting and studying. Last night, I completed my training for Women's circle facilitator. Next I will get
certified in teen's circles, then wedding circles, baby blessing circles and, finally, online circles.

Also I have been journaling, doing daily tea rituals with prayer and herbal tea. I also concentrate on my magic, plus the daily cooking and cleaning. I am actually quite grateful for this opportunity to learn, go with in, meditate and grow and advance spiritually amidst the pandemic.

Thankfully, the weather has still been warm and there is a park right behind our house. So, I go and read about crystals or magic, or self-improvement out there somedays when there is no one around.

We are still in stage 3 lockdown due to Covid-19. Today I participated in a mass meditation to envision all affected people being healed and the coronavirus leaving the planet, as well as any fear and being replaced with love and equality. Also, last Wednesday, I attended a wonderful online circle where we first cleansed ourselves with sage, then placed some relaxing essential oils on our hands, rubbed them together, took three deep breaths and inhaled the scent.

We also have the snowflake obsidian crystal which is for grounding and protection. I have programmed it with my intentions, which were for peace and calm in these crazy times.

This week, I have been studying the Teen circle facilitator online course which I completed yesterday. I received my certification thankfully. I have been getting requests for some online tarot card readings also.

Chapter 7

Focus on growth

Last Wednesday was my birthday. I had a wonderful day. My lovely neighbor gave me some opium perfume. My mum had some beautiful flowers delivered as well as amazing food from Brunettis: arancini for lunch, and potato leek pancetta soup as well as some incredible bread for dinner. We also ate some incredible cakes!

The night of my birthday was also a full pink moon and the largest for the year 2020. I performed a spell for healing and vitality. I was supposed to make a poppet, which is a doll that you add healing herbs and crystals inside, but sewing and cutting skills aren't my best. I accidentally cut the arm off. So, I decided to make a mojo bag instead. A mojo bag is a small bag you put the healing herbs and crystals inside.

As the week has gone on. I also got into my studies and completed my certification as a Wise Woman Circle facilitator, and also a Wedding Circle facilitator.

We are still in lockdown due to Covid-19.

Now, people are speaking of comets and meteorites. This made me reflect on another experience I had years back. I was staying out in the country at a festival where everyone was camping. I recalled standing alone in the field with an alien craft right above me as I was returning home from the festival. I was praying they would take me. I was unsure if this event had been a dream or a real experience, but when I spoke with other people who also had attended this event, they said that they also had seen many spacecraft flying over.

Whether it was real or not, it was an incredible experience.

My dreams leading up to these times were often of the Chinese taking over Australia. The coronavirus was first heard of in Wuhan, China, and that now makes sense as to why I was having these dreams. Just because I was in Australia I have many Chinese friends. As in all races, there are good and not so great people amongst these Chinese.

There is always light and dark. We are all really made from the primordial light.

Last night was the new moon. So I decide to perform a spell for luck. We are still in lockdown and people are saying it may last another month. During this time, I have been horrified at the discovery of Satanic rites and pedophile rings in Hollywood. Now, I'm beginning to understand Ricky Gervass' speech at the Golden Globe Awards. Yet, spiritualists are saying that people are becoming aware of all this, which means that things are making way for all of it to be cleared. I'm hoping that means things will happen to put a stop to it all.

I also recall remembered another amazing experience when I was in Bangkok. I was walking along Khao San road. It is a long street busy with people and market stalls everywhere. An Indian man with a turban approached me and said he wanted to tell me some information. He led me down a side alley that was more secluded or with less people walking around. He took out a piece of paper and a pen he asked me write down the name of someone I loved, a place I loved, a good friend and two other things that were special me. I can't remember exactly what I wrote. He took the paper, folded it and set it alight until there was nothing but ashes. He then took another piece of paper, which was blank, and folded it, closed his eyes, prayed on it, while folding it between his hands in prayer position. Then he opened it and showed it to me.

I was amazed as it had all the answers to the questions I had written in my own handwriting! After this, he told me some predictions for my future.

Lately, during this lockdown, I have been having lots of memories coming back to me. Like, as a child my father calling me kaky handed because I am left handed whereas he was right handed. I also realize that I have always had a love for writing. As I was growing up, I used to write poems. I had a folder (Manila) with pages of typed poems at the age of 15.

Today, I wrote a poem which I asked a friend to name for me. The title she gave it is "Inclination." I give my love and trust freely. Always remaining when unbroken but if broken, in time through prayer, forgiveness, still only giving nothing but love.

I have also recently found someone to collaborate with in hosting an online circle. I have five weeks to prepare. I will be having a twenty minute activity for self-love affirmations in which I will offer as many possible then also give sometime for participants to add any of their own as well.

Also, as of last Friday night, Minister Scott Morrison announced the disbandment of COAG which would essentially put us in a State of Dictatorship. On Monday, I will send a letter by registered mail to the Governor General to say I do not consent!

In this time of pandemic, I have been learning many things. The straw man is a good Youtube video about how we are registered at birth on our birth certificates. The Straw Man claims that we are actually registered as deceased, and making us a slave to the system. Therefore, I have now registered as a living sovereign being. It doesn't cost to do so, in case any of you my readers also wish to do the same.

Thankfully, some of my work is starting up again. There was a full moon, so I performed a forgiveness spell and meditation as this is the perfect time for giving forgiveness and letting go. The New Moon, however, is about whatever you want to bring into your life.

I have also discovered an upcoming summit, which is planning a global class action against the COVID-19 lockdown and forced vaccinations. I wish to be part of this. It will be held during the weekend of 20 and 21 June 2020. I definitely will be attending online, so I have volunteered with the common law courts to be a bailiff.

Chapter 8

Take care of You

We are still in the midst of the time of Covid-19 or the pandemic, which is a distraction from fundamental truths of common law or lore. I have been using the time constructively and working with my magic and meditation as well as gratitude practice.

I have, on the Full Moon, written and burnt to release and let go of anyone I felt I needed to forgive. I have also decorated my magical broom as well as walked in the park and found the perfect stick to create my own magical crystal wand with. I simply used a glue gun to attach my crystals, each of which has a colour corresponding to each chakra. I also created a manifestation spray which smells amazing using herbs or basil and mint as well aromatherapy oils of vanilla Pachouli. These are great for luck and abundance, and also already blended abundance oil.

On Instagram, I had seen one of the witches I follow has become a brand rep for a wonderful magical product. I thought I would love to do the same. So I messaged the company, to which they replied saying they had all the brand reps they need for now, but I'm welcome to apply the next time they advertise.

The following evening, another wonderful magic supplies company had an ad looking for brand reps so I applied and the next day I was told I would be accepted to be their brand rep, so my manifestation spray is really working a treat.

All my work has been cut short due to COVID-19, but, thankfully, I have been getting clients for phone and video call readings, which I am able to do from anywhere as long as I have my tarot cards with me.

I have been having lots of dreams of Agni Hotra, all of which have felt lovely to wake from. Still in Covid times, but my last few days have been filled with more magic, performing spells, writing gratitude, journaling and meditation.

Another story I wanted to share was in the time of living in the shared house with seven other people. I had written a submission to apply as a chakra dance teacher in Sydney. I had to travel to Sydney to take part in a chakra dance class to see if it truly what was I wanted to do.

So, I booked my Chakra Dance class and ticket and was scheduled to travel at the end of the week. However, I became extremely ill that week. I think it was gastro. I couldn't stop throwing up and going to the toilet. I felt so weak so I just slept for ages. I felt like I was going to die. One morning I awoke feeling a little better. So I decided to walk to the shop and buy vegetables to cook roasted and get a juice with as much fruit and veg in it as possible. I needed to do this to try and get some vitamins and minerals into my system. Again I awoke feeling much better, and it was the day to travel to Sydney for chakra dance class.

Thankfully, I was up for the journey. I made it to Sydney and was staying with family. Once again, thankfully, the class wasn't till the following day. So, I had more time with family and to rest and to heal a little bit more. The morning of my class, I was feeling much better. I caught the train on time and attended the chakra dance class, which I thoroughly enjoyed.

It was a beautiful sunny day on my way back to my family's place. At the station, I could see an amazing view of the Sydney Opera house and Sydney Harbour Bridge, which my father told me my grandfather put the first pins in when it was being built. The day was stunning, and the view was spectacular. Better yet, the chakra dance class was amazing. I felt wonderful.

Chapter 9

Kindness matters

I was feeling so blessed, grateful and amazing thinking to myself life is incredible with all its highs and lows, from feeling like I was at deaths door to feeling amazing, full of life and energy.

Another amazing experience I had when I was in India was when I had a long-distance train ride with Guru. We met a very interesting woman with whom we struck a conversation while journeying.

She was some sort of historian who worked at the Ghandi Ashram. She was telling us that there was a time in history that she knew of when both the Bible and the Koran had been edited and altered at the same time. It was fascinating listening to her as she knew so much about many religions.

Back again now to the current time of Covid-19: Daily I have been keeping up my ascension meditations as this is the time of the great awakening. I continue my daily practice of writing a gratitude list for the day working giving tarot readings, and also keeping up my magical practices.

In this past week, I performed a forgiveness meditation or spell as well as a love spells to my inner child. In this time of Covid and isolation, I have had many epiphanies or awakenings. One of the things I meditated on is that, even though we are all separate beings on this earth, we are all in truth interconnected. My mask says #WWG1WGA which means where we go one we go all. It means that, whatever affects one person, in reality affects us all. My eyes have been opened to so many horrific acts that have been happening with paedophilia and child sex trafficking, thankfully not first-hand, but through so many wonderful souls working tirelessly to stop it from happening.

This Full Moon I didn't have the energy for performing magic, so I meditated, journaled and spent time connecting with people in my life that I love and inspire me.

The jurisdiction of the Australian government has been challenged and publicly denied. If the Australian government cannot provide evidence of a lawful sovereignty, then it is not a lawful government. Are you willing to accept a government with no lawful authority? I'm sure not many others aren't either.

Jurisdiction is essential. The truth will set you free. Let's confront it and end this madness #peopletreaty: this is what I support. True sovereignty must be restored, not just in this country but all other countries as well.

Today, it is the Lion's gate portal. It opened on the 26 July and continues until the 12th August. Beams of high vibrational energy come to planet earth in this time. In numerology, the 8th day of the 8th month is a highly spiritual and changed time. The number 8 represents infinity, the infinite soul that we are and the infinite journey that we take. It represents the "forever consciousness part of the soul, the soul that has lived and will continue to live long after and long before this incarnation.

Today, I sat for Gabby Bernstein's appreciation meditation, and meditated and journaled about everything I am grateful for, which at this point in my life is a lot. Although my life has been challenging at times, I'm grateful for all the experience I have been through so far and the strength and wisdom I have gained. After completing the appreciation meditation and journaling, I'm now performing my own tea ceremony with 2 very berry fruit tea, made of hibiscus and raspberry. I am saying a prayer whilst in enjoying the tea.

This tea also has antioxidant which improves immune system and circulation, and lowers cholesterol as well as aids digestion and increases metabolism,

By the way, raspberry tea is not advisable for pregnant women, as well as hibiscus tea.

Throughout the entire time of the pandemic I have got qualified in hosting circles. I'm also now a qualified yoga teacher and I'm now qualified to host cacao ceremonies. Through the lineage of the Seven Rays from the Andes. How amazing to have learnt ceremonial arts via online with such incredibly special beings.

Now that I have shared my story with you, I hope that you have picked up some inspiration. I wish all beings everywhere to be well, be safe, be happy, be loved, and evolve into Happy, Blessed, peaceful, and amazingly special unique beings.

In the time it has taken me to prepare this book. I have also completed 200 hour yoga teacher training with Akasha online which I highly recommend. As well I have completed my trainings in sacred cacao ceremonies from the lineage of the seven rays. My love and passion for learning about healing, meditation and magic is still ongoing and I doubt it will ever cease.

Wishing everyone lots of love and light in your life from my heart to yours. I am another you, In LAKECH which means I am another yourself. Blessed Be.

-THE END-

CPSIA information can be obtained
at www.ICGtesting.com
Printed in the USA
BVHW092324060922
646316BV00012B/740